Destina
Detectives

India

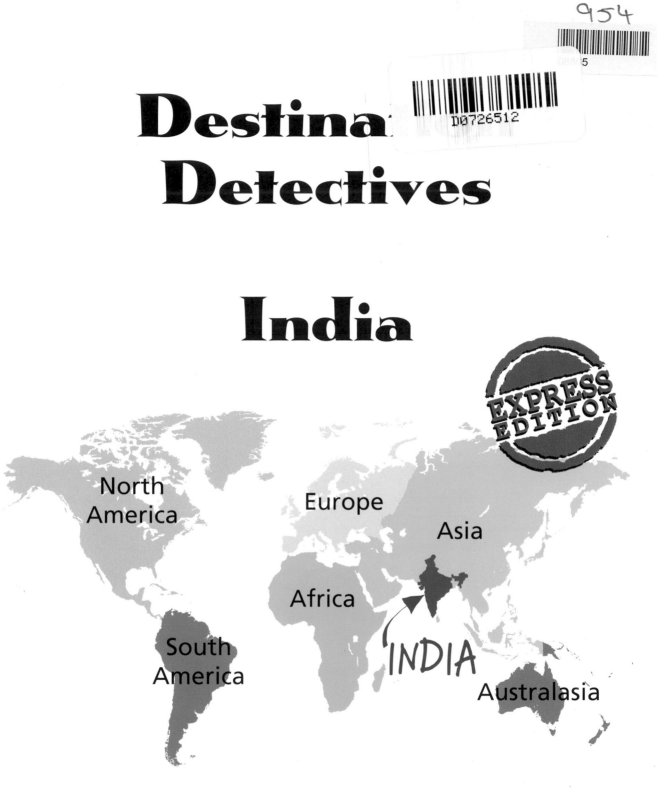

North America

Europe

Asia

Africa

South America

INDIA

Australasia

Anita Roy

Raintree

www.raintreepublishers.co.uk
Visit our website to find out more information about **Raintree** books.

To order:
☎ Phone 44 (0) 1865 888112
🖹 Send a fax to 44 (0) 1865 314091
💻 Visit the Raintree Bookshop at **www.raintreepublishers.co.uk** to browse our catalogue and order online.

First published in Great Britain by
Raintree, Halley Court, Jordan Hill,
Oxford OX2 8EJ, part of Harcourt Education.
Raintree is a registered trademark of Harcourt
Education Ltd.

Produced for Raintree Publishers by Discovery Books Ltd
Editorial: Kathryn Walker, Melanie Copland, and Lucy Beevor
Design: Victoria Bevan, Rob Norridge, and Kamae Design
Picture Research: Hannah Taylor and Kay Altwegg
Production: Duncan Gilbert
Originated by Dot Gradations
Printed and bound in China
by South China Printing Company

10 digit ISBN 1 406 20401 3 (hardback)
13 digit ISBN 978 1 406 20401 8
10 09 08 07 06
10 9 8 7 6 5 4 3 2 1

10 digit ISBN 1 406 20408 0 (paperback)
13 digit ISBN 978 1 406 20408 7
10 09 08 07 06
10 9 8 7 6 5 4 3 2 1

British Library Cataloguing in Publication Data
Roy, Anita
India. – (Destination Detectives)
954'.0531
A full catalogue record for this book is available from
the British Library.

This levelled text is a version of *Freestyle:
Destination Detectives: India*

Acknowledgements
Alamy Images pp. 32 (Barend Gerr), 29 (david sanger photography), 20 (dubassy), 12–13 (easywind), 24–25 (Fabrice Bettex), 19l (Fiona Jeffrey), 23t (Helene Rogers), 4–5 (PCL), 28r (Peter Adams Photography); Bridgeman Art Library p. 19r; Corbis pp. 43 (Adam Woolfitt), 21 (Angelo Hornak), 36 (Catherine Karnow), 39 (David Samuel Robbins), pp. 23b, 40l (Earl & Nazima Kowall), 42l (Elio Ciol), 16 (Enzo & Paolo Ragazzini), 18 (Gian Berto Vanni), pp. 9, 10–11, 27, 34–35, 40r (Jeremy Horner), 6t (Jim Zuckerman), pp. 6bl, 24, 41 (Lindsay Hebberd), pp. 22, 6br (Reuters), 37 (Reuters/Arko Datta), 38 (Reuters/Javanta Shaw), 34 (Ted Streshinsky); Corbis Royalty Free 17l; Getty Images pp. 25 (AFP), pp. 17r, 42r (Photodisc), Harcourt Education Ltd pp. 13, 15, 33l, 33r (Rob Bowden/ EASI-Images), 28l (Sharron Lovell); Magnum Photos p. 14 (Ian Berry); Panos Pictures p. 11 (Karen Robinson), pp. 5, 31 (Mark Henley); Photolibrary.com p. 26; Rex Features p. 12; Robert Harding pp. 8–9 (Sybil Sassoon).

Cover photograph of brightly coloured spices reproduced with permission of Getty Images/Photodisc.

Every effort has been made to contact copyright holders of any material reproduced in this book. Any omissions will be rectified in subsequent printings if notice is given to the publishers.

The paper used to print this book comes from sustainable resources.

Contents

Any words appearing in the text in bold, **like this,** are explained in the glossary. You can also look out for them in the Word Bank at the bottom of each page.

Where in the world?

India at your doorstep

Many Indians buy their daily supplies from people pushing carts in the street. These handcarts are piled with fruit, vegetables, buckets, and mops. The cry of the *sabji-wallah* (vegetable seller) is a familiar sound throughout India.

You wake up to the sound of a street seller shouting "*Sabji*!" (vegetables). Sparrows twitter and parakeets screech. The sun is shining. The air is warm and breezy.

You step outside. You see a group of children covered with paint. They yell "Happy Holi!" and throw coloured powder paint at you. Some squirt you with water. They are celebrating the spring festival of Holi (see page 24). You are in India.

The festival of Holi celebrates the beginning of spring. It is also known as the "festival of colours".

➤

WORD BANK fort specially strengthened building designed to defend an area in wartime

There are more than a billion people in India. This is nearly one-sixth of the world's population. India is a huge country to explore.

Your starting point is the capital city of Delhi. Will you go:

- north to the snow-topped Himalayan mountains?
- west to see the camels and **forts** of Rajasthan?
- south to the coconut groves of Kerala?
- east to explore the countryside of Bengal and the busy city of Kolkata (Calcutta)?

A tale of two cities

Delhi is actually two cities in one. Old Delhi dates back to 1638. New Delhi was built in the early 1900s. At that time India was part of the British **Empire**. The British rulers built New Delhi to be the capital city.

This is the Rashtrapati Bhavan. It is the president's house in Delhi.

empire country or group of countries ruled over by another country

A varied land

The "Seven Sisters"

Some of India's most beautiful scenery is in the northeast. The seven states in this region are almost cut off from the rest of India. These states are known as the "Seven Sisters". Most people who live there are from different **tribes**. Each tribe has its own customs and style of dress.

You look at a map of the country. India is huge. It is about a third of the size of the United States. India is made up of 28 states and 7 union territories. You must decide where to visit first. You read your guidebook and add labels to the map. These labels will help you decide.

These women wear embroidered ghagra (skirts) and choli (blouses). Tiny mirrors decorate these clothes.

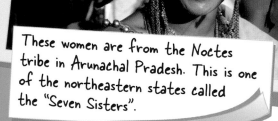

These women are from the Noctes tribe in Arunachal Pradesh. This is one of the northeastern states called the "Seven Sisters".

The Punjab in north-west India has good farming land.

WORD BANK   tribe group of people who live together and share the same language and customs

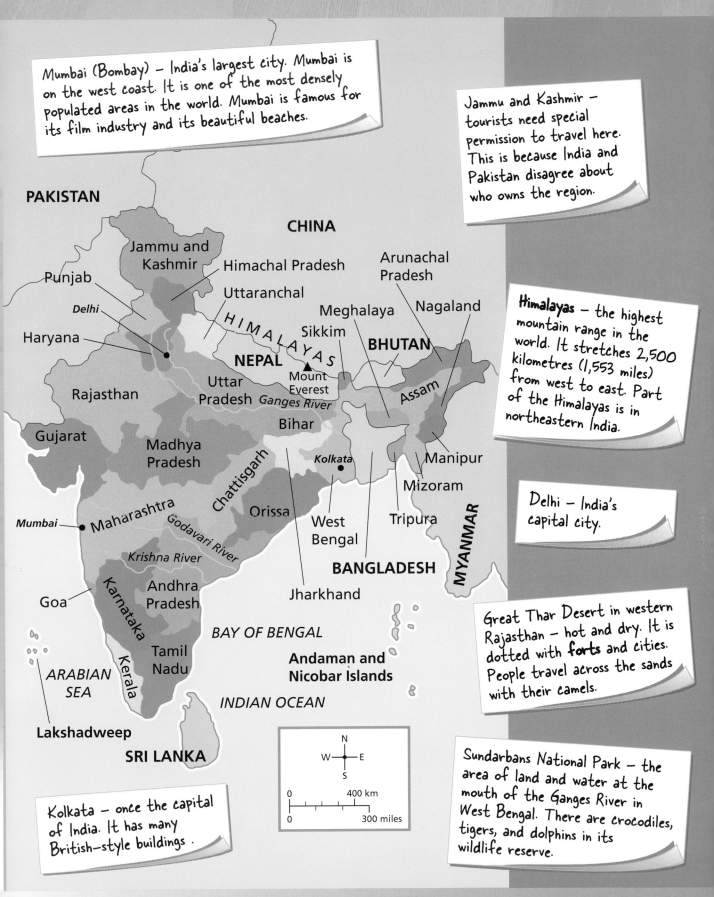

Mumbai (Bombay) – India's largest city. Mumbai is on the west coast. It is one of the most densely populated areas in the world. Mumbai is famous for its film industry and its beautiful beaches.

Jammu and Kashmir – tourists need special permission to travel here. This is because India and Pakistan disagree about who owns the region.

PAKISTAN

CHINA

Jammu and Kashmir

Himachal Pradesh

Arunachal Pradesh

Punjab

Uttaranchal

Meghalaya

Nagaland

Delhi

Haryana

HIMALAYAS

Sikkim

BHUTAN

NEPAL

Rajasthan

Uttar Pradesh

Mount Everest

Ganges River

Assam

Bihar

Gujarat

Madhya Pradesh

Chattisgarh

Kolkata

Manipur

Mumbai

Maharashtra

Godavari River

Orissa

Mizoram

West Bengal

Tripura

MYANMAR

Krishna River

BANGLADESH

Goa

Andhra Pradesh

Jharkhand

Karnataka

BAY OF BENGAL

Kerala

Tamil Nadu

Andaman and Nicobar Islands

ARABIAN SEA

INDIAN OCEAN

Lakshadweep

SRI LANKA

Himalayas – the highest mountain range in the world. It stretches 2,500 kilometres (1,553 miles) from west to east. Part of the Himalayas is in northeastern India.

Delhi – India's capital city.

Great Thar Desert in western Rajasthan – hot and dry. It is dotted with **forts** and cities. People travel across the sands with their camels.

Sundarbans National Park – the area of land and water at the mouth of the Ganges River in West Bengal. There are crocodiles, tigers, and dolphins in its wildlife reserve.

Kolkata – once the capital of India. It has many British-style buildings.

N
W E
S

0   400 km

0   300 miles

fort specially strengthened building designed to defend an area in wartime

Geography

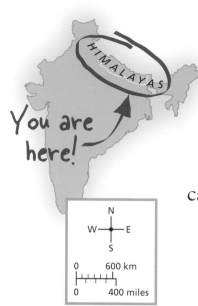

HIMALAYAS

You are here!

N
W — E
S

0   600 km
0   400 miles

It is beginning to get hot in Delhi. You decide to head for the hills. You drive for five hours across flat **plains**. Finally, you see mountains in the distance.

The air gets cooler as the road winds upward. The views are wonderful. There are forests and waterfalls. In the distance you can see the snow-capped Himalayan mountains.

Hill stations

There are many pretty villages and towns on the lower slopes of the Himalayas. This kind of settlement is called a **hill station**. In the 1900s, many British people made their summer homes in hill stations. You can still see these British-style buildings.

The Darjeeling Himalayan Railway started running in 1881. It is so slow that you can hop off the train on one bend and walk to catch it up at the next.

WORD BANK   plain large, flat area of land

The **Himalayas** have some of the highest peaks on Earth. These include Kanchenjunga, K2, and Mount Everest. The mountains separate India from its northern neighbours.

Many Indians believe the Himalayas are holy mountains. You can see temples and shrines everywhere. The air is clear and the views are stunning. Some people call it "Heaven on Earth".

Kanchenjunga is the highest mountain in the Indian Himalayas. It is the third highest in the world.

hill station small town or village high up in the hills

Rivers

Many of India's rivers start from the **Himalayas**. They include the Brahmaputra, the Indus, the Yamuna, and the Ganges rivers.

The Ganges is the holiest river of all. In India it is called *Ma Ganga*. The Ganges starts high up in an ice cave in the Himalayas. It flows down through the **plains** and towards the eastern coast.

Rivers of life

The government has built huge dams along India's rivers. These dams use the flow of the waters to produce electricity. India has more than 3,300 big dams.

Women gather on the banks of the Ganges to wash and offer prayers to the holy river.

WORD BANK   Hinduism   religion that started in India. It involves the worship of many gods and goddesses.

All along the banks of the Ganges you see people washing clothes, bathing, or praying. **Hinduism** is the main religion in India. **Hindus** believe that the water of the Ganges is **holy**. They believe that the river washes away **sins**. Sins are bad deeds that go against a religion's teachings.

Think carefully before taking a dip though. The lower stretches of the Ganges are highly **polluted**. Nearly 1 billion litres (2.1 billion pints) of waste goes into the river every day.

Rivers of death

Many people are against building dams. They believe that the dams cause too much damage. Many people have lost their homes and land in floods caused by the dams.

Villagers in the central state of Madhya Pradesh cling to their homes. The waters rise around them after a dam was built on the Narmada River.

polluted when air, water, or soil has been made dirty or harmful by waste or chemicals

Plains, coasts, and islands

South of the **Himalayas**, the landscape changes. A huge area of flat and **fertile** land covers central-northern India. Many plants and crops grow here. This region is known as the Indo-Gangetic **Plains**.

South of the plains, the land rises into a rocky **plateau**. This high, flat land covers much of southern India. It is called the Deccan Plateau. There are hills on either side of the plateau. These hills run alongside the coastline.

Whole villages were destroyed in the tsunami of December 2004.

The Andaman Islands are famous for their beautiful beaches.

WORD BANK   fertile good for growing crops and other types of plants

You decide to explore some beaches. You fly to Mumbai in western India (see map on page 7). Then you take a train further south. You see miles of sandy beaches lined with coconut palms.

India also has two sets of islands (see map on page 7). To the west are the Lakshadweep Islands. To the east are the Andaman and Nicobar Islands. Both eastern sets of islands are home to many rare birds, fish, and plants.

Gone fishing

There are many tiny fishing villages dotted along the Indian coasts. The fishermen set out in traditional boats to bring in the daily haul of fish. The fishermen in the photo below use nets made from bamboo and rope.

plateau area of flat land that is higher than the surrounding land

Climate

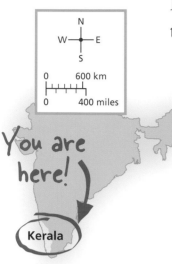

You are here!

Kerala

It gets hotter and stickier the further south you travel. As the summer gets hotter, people look forward to the **monsoon**. The monsoon is the rainy season that lasts from June to the end of September.

You keep travelling south to the state of Kerala. When you get there, the first drops of rain start to fall. Everyone rushes out of their houses to celebrate.

Children dance with joy as the monsoon begins. They live in Cherrapunji in the northeastern state of Meghalaya. This is the wettest place on Earth!

WORD BANK   monsoon rainy season, from June to September

India needs the rain that the monsoon brings. About 80 percent of the year's rainfall happens in the monsoon months. A good monsoon means healthy crops. A bad one can mean **starvation**.

There is a lot of different weather in India. The wettest place in the world is in northeastern India. One of the driest places on Earth is the Great Thar Desert in the northwest of India.

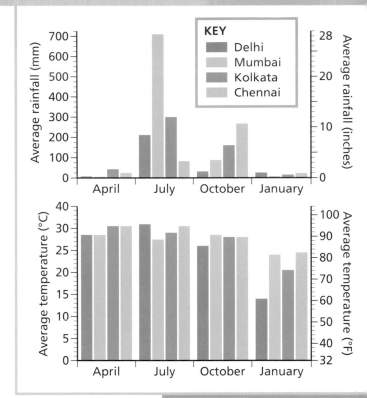

Farmers grow crops in even the driest, hottest areas of India.

starvation lack of basic food needed to survive

Wildlife

The **monsoon** season is over. It is now cooler and easier to travel. You decide to leave Kerala. You want to see some of India's wildlife.

On safari

You travel by train to Katni in central India. Then you take a long bus ride to Bandhavgarh National Park.

At Bandhavgarh, you set off through the jungle on an elephant safari. Monkeys clamber about in the trees. Deer wander in the forest. You even hear the roar of a tiger.

Tigers under threat

India used to have thousands of tigers. Today, there are only a few hundred left. Many tigers have been killed by hunters. Humans have taken over huge areas of their natural **habitat**. National parks like Bandhavgarh have been set up to protect these wonderful animals.

Elephant workers

Did you know that the Indian government employs animals? Indian elephants are still used to carry mail to remote corners of the country.

◄ People have worked with elephants for thousands of years. This elephant is using its trunk to move heavy logs.

WORD BANK   habitat   natural home of animals and plants

It is now against the law to hunt tigers in India. But hunters are still killing tigers. Some people will pay large amounts of money for tiger skins and body parts.

The sacred snake

Hindus believe that snakes are holy animals. Many of their gods are pictured with snakes. There is even a festival where snakes are offered milk, honey, and flowers.

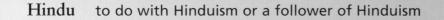

India is one of the world's oldest civilizations. Cities existed in northern India over 4,000 years ago! India has many historical places to visit.

Sanchi

Sanchi attracts visitors from around the world. It is in the central state of Madhya Pradesh. Sanchi is the site of many **Buddhist** temples and **monuments**. There are large, dome-shaped buildings in honour of Buddha. There is also a famous pillar carved with four lions. These lions have become India's **emblem**. They appear on India's rupee coin.

The lion pillar was built by King Ashoka. Ashoka was a ruler of the Mauryan **Empire**. The Mauryan Empire once covered most of what is now India.

Gateway of India

India was ruled by the British from 1757 to 1947. In 1924, the British finished building the Gateway to India (see right). This huge archway is Mumbai's most famous monument.

WORD BANK   monument important historic site or a structure built to honour a special person or event

Hampi

Further south in Karnataka state lies the ancient city of Hampi. It was the heart of the Vijayanagara Empire. This empire lasted for more than 300 years. When the city was conquered in 1565, it took more than 6 months to carry away all its treasures.

Buildings of the Mughal

The Mughal emperors ruled most of India during the 16th and 17th centuries. The Mughal emperor Shah Jahan (see picture below) built India's most famous building, the Taj Mahal (see page 42).

This is the Narasimha shrine in Hampi. It was carved from a single boulder!

emblem object used as a symbol for a place, person, or thing

Hinduism

Hindus believe in **reincarnation**. This means that after you die your soul is reborn in another body. Good things that you do in this life count towards a good next life.

Religion

Religion is very important for most Indians. There are many different religions in India. The chart on the right shows what percentage of the population follows each religion.

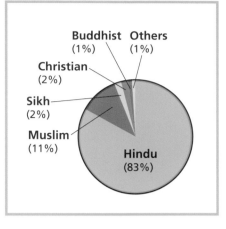

Buddhist (1%)
Others (1%)
Christian (2%)
Sikh (2%)
Muslim (11%)
Hindu (83%)

A Hindu *mandir* (temple) is in honour of one god or goddess. This statue of Shiva, the destroyer, sits in the Chattarpur *Mandir* in New Delhi.

WORD BANK   reincarnation rebirth of the soul into another body

Hinduism

An ordinary **Hindu** house is full of pictures of gods. They appear in paintings, on calendars, and as little statues.

Hindu prayer ceremonies are called *poojas*. They are performed at weddings, funerals, and for new babies. Some people do small *poojas* as part of their daily routine. They offer flowers, burn incense, and chant prayers.

Hindu gods

There are many Hindu gods and goddesses. The main ones are:

Brahma – the creator

Vishnu – the preserver

Shiva – the destroyer.

The fierce goddess Kali is shown here. She is dancing on the corpse of one of her victims.

Hindu to do with Hinduism or a follower of Hinduism

Islam

Islam is the second biggest religion in India. Followers of Islam are called **Muslims**. They believe in one god, Allah. They also believe that Allah chose the **prophet** Muhammad to spread his word. Muslim places of worship are called **mosques**.

Five times a day, thousands of Muslims gather to pray at the Jama Masjid in Delhi. This is India's largest mosque.

WORD BANK   prophet someone chosen by a god to tell people what the god wants them to do

> Guru Nanak was the founder of the Sikh religion. His picture is kept in many Sikh homes.

Buddhism

Buddhism was founded by Siddhartha Gautama. He was born in Nepal in 563 BC but spent most of his life in India. Siddhartha became known as the Buddha. Buddhism teaches people that perfect happiness is found through **wisdom** and understanding.

Sikhism

A small percentage of Indians are **Sikhs**. You can recognize Sikh men by their beards and turbans. Turbans are headdresses made of long pieces of cloth. Most Sikhs are from the state of Punjab in northern India. They believe in one God.

> These young monks are studying. They are in one of the ancient **Buddhist** temples of Ladakh in northern India.

Christianity

Most Indian Christians live in the southern states of Kerala and Goa. Goa was ruled by the Portuguese for more than 450 years. The Portuguese came from western Europe. They built some beautiful churches in Goa.

Buddhist to do with Buddhism or a follower of Buddhism

Festival fun

Gods and demons

Dussehra is a popular Hindu festival. It celebrates the victory of the god Rama over the demon king Ravana. At the end of Dussehra, huge models of Ravana and his brothers are set on fire (see below).

There always seems to be a festival happening in India. Some festivals celebrate the seasons. There is a spring festival called Holi (see page 4) and an autumn harvest festival of Pongal. At Pongal, people decorate their cows with flowers and paint.

A festival feast

The main **Muslim** festival is Eid. It marks the end of the month of Ramadan (or Ramzan). During Ramadan, Muslims do not eat between sunrise and sunset. They celebrate the end of Ramadan with prayers, presents, and fabulous food.

 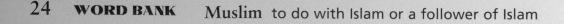 **WORD BANK**   Muslim to do with Islam or a follower of Islam

Festival of light

The biggest festival of the year is the **Hindu** festival of Diwali. People decorate their houses with lights, candles, and lamps. These lights are to welcome the goddess Lakshmi into homes. Lakshmi is the Hindu goddess of wealth. When it gets dark, the fireworks begin.

Huge displays of fireworks and lights mark the Hindu festival of Diwali.

Rangolis

Rangolis are colourful patterns made on the floor during festivals (below). At Diwali, Hindus draw *rangolis* to encourage the goddess Lakshmi to enter their homes.

Everyday life

In Kerala, you ate crispy pancakes and rice cakes with coconut chutney. Now you are back in northern India. You notice that the food here is very different.

Roadside snacks

There are many roadside cafes called *dhabas*. You decide to stop at one and try some *parathas*. These are fried flatbreads stuffed with spiced vegetables. You also try a cup of *chai*. *Chai* is tea boiled up with milk, sugar, and spices.

A *thali* is a tray with different foods in little bowls. This allows you to mix and match flavours.

Throughout northern India there are all kinds of tasty snacks sold on the streets. These snacks are called *chaat*. They are served on little leaf bowls.

A sweet tooth

Indians are very fond of sweet foods. Many of them are made with milk. These might be crunchy *jalebis*. *Jalebis* are tubes of fried batter that drip with sugar syrup. Or they might be *barfi*. This is a fudge-like sweet made with cashew nuts. Just take your pick!

A *dhaba* selling potato cakes served with mango and chilli sauce. This is just one of the many snacks sold on India's streets.

Finger-licking good

Eating with your hands is the best way to eat Indian food. It takes a bit of practice though. But remember that it is bad manners to eat with your left hand.

Clothing

In a big city like Delhi, lots of people wear western-style clothes. Many people wear trousers and shirts, or dresses or skirts. But in the smaller towns and villages, more people wear traditional Indian clothes.

Elegant dressing

Indian women often wear *salwar kameez*. This is a loose trouser suit. It is worn with a long scarf around the shoulders. Women also wear saris. A sari is a long piece of cloth that is wound around the body and draped over one shoulder.

One of the most expensive of all saris are *kanjivaram* saris. Real gold thread is often woven into the silk cloth.

➤

Traditional menswear

You might think pyjamas are just what you wear in bed. In fact the word comes from India. Indian men often wear loose cotton trousers called *pajamas*. They wear them under long shirts called *kurtas*.

In some parts of India, men also wear the *lungi* or the *dhoti*. Both of these garments are lengths of cloth folded and wrapped around the waist.

This man from northern India wears *kurta pajamas* made of homespun cotton.

Life in an Indian city

Delhi is India's capital city. But in the past, Calcutta was the capital. It is now called Kolkata. You decide to see what the city of Kolkata is like.

Your train pulls into Howrah station. The first thing you notice is the huge numbers of people. The platform is packed. There are porters carrying luggage. There are beggars, travellers, and people selling things.

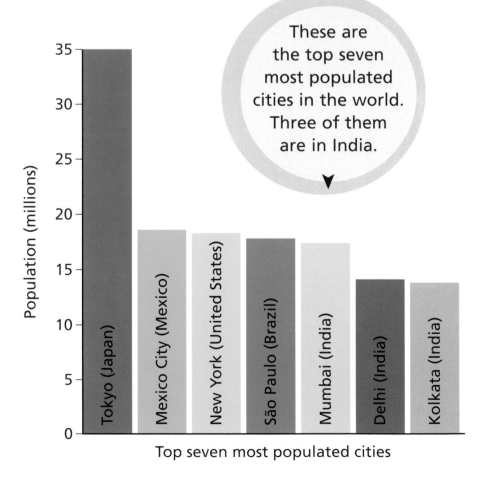

You are here!

Kolkata

N
W — E
S

0   600 km

0   400 miles

City slums

Many Indian cities have large **slums**. Slums are dirty and overcrowded areas where poor people live. Dharavi slum in Mumbai is the largest in Asia. It houses about 1 million people. It has no sewers or running water.

These are the top seven most populated cities in the world. Three of them are in India.

Population (millions)

35
30
25
20
15
10
5
0

Tokyo (Japan)
Mexico City (Mexico)
New York (United States)
São Paulo (Brazil)
Mumbai (India)
Delhi (India)
Kolkata (India)

Top seven most populated cities

rickshaw small vehicle for carrying people and goods. Some are pulled by hand, others are pedalled or motorised.

You have to cross the Hooghly River to get to the main city. You take a taxi across Howrah Bridge. Two million people cross this bridge every day.

You see all kinds of traffic on Kolkata's streets. There are cars, horse-drawn carts, and small vehicles called **rickshaws**. Some rickshaws are motorised. Others are pulled by bicycles or people. There are dogs, cows, and sometimes even elephants on the streets.

Kolkata's streets are crowded, noisy, and chaotic.

slum area populated by very poor people, where the conditions are dirty and overcrowded

Life in an Indian village

Most Indians do not live in cities. Seventy-three percent live in the countryside. Their lives are centred around the changing seasons. The villagers depend on their crops for food.

The green countryside of west Bengal is not far from Kolkata. Heavy rainfall and a warm climate mean that everything grows well here. There are small villages with huts made of mud and straw. Every village has fish ponds. This is because fish are an important food in Bengal.

Open-air classes

Village schools in India usually have no chairs, tables, or books. Sometimes there is not even a building. Children sit outdoors and use chalk to write on boards (see right).

oxen   male cattle

Animals are an important part of village life. Male cattle called **oxen** are used to plough the fields. Cows and water buffalos give milk. Chickens are raised for eggs and meat.

Villagers travel around on bicycles or carts pulled by water buffalos. West Bengal has a rainy climate so it usually has enough water. In drier parts of India, women might have to walk for miles to fetch water.

Collecting and carrying water is seen as a woman's job. These young women are carrying clay water pots on their heads.

Buffalos and cows are very important to country life. Both animals give milk. They are also used for ploughing fields and pulling carts.

Culture and Sport

As you travel around India, you realize that music is an important part of Indian life. It may be songs from the latest hit film. It may be religious chants. Where there's music, there's also dance.

Kathakali

The oldest form of Indian dance is called *Kathakali*. It comes from the southwestern state of Kerala. *Kathakali* is danced only by men. The dancers dress in spectacular costumes and wear mask-like make up.

A classical note

The sitar is a long-necked instrument with up to twenty strings. The most famous sitar player is Pandit Ravi Shankar (see below). His music is known throughout the world.

These *Kathakali* dancers are from Kerala. The villain's face is painted black. The hero's is green.

WORD BANK Hindu to do with Hinduism or a follower of Hinduism

Bharata Natyam

Bharata Natyam is another ancient dance form. Unlike *Kathakali*, it is performed mainly by women. The dancer uses her eyes, face, and fingers to tell a **Hindu** story. Each movement of the hand has a different meaning. The dancer wears bells around her ankles. They jingle as she dances.

Folk dance

Each different region of India has its own folk dances and songs. These dances are part of special celebrations such as weddings and festivals.

Hooray for Bollywood!

Every small town in India has its own cinema. Indian film stars are treated almost like gods. Wherever they go, huge crowds gather to see them.

India's film industry produces over 800 new films each year. This is far more than the US film industry. But Indian blockbusters are much cheaper to produce than ones from Hollywood.

Huge billboards advertising the latest hit films are often painted by hand.

Mumbai (Bombay) is where most of the films are produced. The Mumbai film industry is often called "Bollywood". The largest numbers of films are in the Hindi language. They combine song, dance, romance, comedy, and lots of action.

Music is a very important part of all Bollywood films. Cassettes and CDs of film music sometimes bring in more money than the ticket sales.

The most popular movie ever!

The most popular Bollywood film of all time is *Dilwale Dulhania Le Jayenge*. It is a story of an Indian living in the United States who falls in love with an Indian girl back home. The movie has been running non-stop for more than 10 years in Mumbai.

Hrishita Bhat (right) dances in the Bollywood movie *Kisna*. The movie was shot in 2004.

Sport and leisure

Many Indians like to spend their free time going to the cinema, watching cricket matches, and going to restaurants. They also like to visit each other's houses to chat and eat.

Cricket

Cricket is played with a bat, a ball, and eleven players on each side. India is cricket mad! Everywhere you go there are kids playing cricket in the streets. But the streets are empty on the day of an important match. Then everyone is watching the match on television or listening to it on the radio.

Indian batsman Sachin Tendulkar (right) in action. This picture shows him playing against South Africa in 2004.

Kabaddi

Kabaddi is a sport played with two teams. A team member rushes into his opponents' half of the field. He tries to touch as many of their team as possible and return to his half in one breath. His opponents try to stop him from returning to his own half.

Carrom

You often see groups of men playing *carrom* on street corners. *Carrom* is played at a square table with a pocket at each corner. Players try to flick flat disks into these pockets.

A group of boys play *carrom* on a street in West Bengal.

Getting out and about

Extreme India!

There are plenty of opportunities for adventure in India. The **Himalayas** offer white-water rafting (below), kayaking, rock climbing, trekking (hiking), and paragliding. In Rajasthan you can trek into the desert on a camel.

Travelling around India by bus can be slow and uncomfortable. Travelling by plane is quicker, but not much fun. The best way to explore India is to travel by train.

Train travel

As you travel back from Kolkata to Delhi you can see the changing scenery from your window. At each station, people rush through the carriage selling *chai* (tea), soap, pens, and snacks. In the evening you fold the seats down to make beds.

Men sell fresh food to passengers as a train stops at Agra in Uttar Pradesh.

Sometimes a single journey can take several days. Travelling in a group is a great way of meeting people. By the end of your journey you will have made lots of friends.

A waiter serves passengers on board the Palace on Wheels. Travelling on this luxury train is very expensive.

Palace on Wheels

The Palace on Wheels is one of the world's most luxurious trains. The train starts from Delhi and takes passengers to Rajasthan's top tourist spots.

The Taj Mahal

Your visit is almost over. But before you leave, you must visit the Taj Mahal. This is India's most famous landmark, and one of the wonders of the world.

The Taj Mahal was built by the Mughal emperor Shah Jahan in the 1700s century. He built it as a monument to his dead wife, Mumtaz Mahal.

Delicate carving

The decorative screens of the Taj Mahal (pictured below) are carved from single blocks of marble. The carvings let in the light and air. They also cast beautiful patterns on the floors.

The Taj Mahal is surrounded by peaceful gardens. ⌄

WORD BANK monument important historic site or a structure built to honour a special person or event

You take the train from Delhi to Agra. Agra is in the neighbouring state of Uttar Pradesh. There you spend the day admiring this amazing building. It is built of white marble. Delicate patterns of semi-precious stones decorate its walls. These semi-precious stones include turquoise, jade, and coral.

Now you have seen the Taj Mahal. But there are plenty of wonderful sights you have not visited yet. It could take you a lifetime to see all the wonders of India.

Final resting place
Shah Jahan planned to build a copy of the Taj Mahal in black marble. But he died before he could start it. Shah Jahan is buried alongside his wife in the Taj Mahal.

This is the ancient Sun Temple at Konark in the southern state of Orissa. It was built in the mid-13th century.

Find out more

World Wide Web

If you want to find out more about India, you can search the Internet using keywords such as these:

- India
- River Ganges
- Hinduism

You can also find your own keywords by using words from this book. Try using a search directory such as **www.yahooligans. com.**

Movies

Monsoon Wedding (2002)
This hit movie is a mixture of English and Hindi.

Kabhi Kushi Kabhie Gham (2001)
Top Indian stars feature in this blockbuster.

You can find out more about India using the books, websites, and addresses listed below:

The Indian Embassy

The Indian Embassy in your own country has lots of information about India. The UK embassy website address is: **www.indianembassy.co.uk**

You can also write to the High Commission of India for more information at the following address:

High Commission of India
India House,
Aldwych,
London WC2B 4NA.

Further reading

Ancient India: People of the Ancient World, Virginia Schomp (Franklin Watts, 2005)

Cooking the Indian Way, Vijay Madavan (Lerner Publishing Company, 2003)

India: Eyewitness Guides, Manini Chatterjee and Anita Roy (Dorling Kindersley, 2002)

WORD BANK   empire country or group of countries ruled over by another country

Timeline

2300 BC
People settle in the Indus Valley in northern India.

1500–800 BC
People arrive in India from Central Asia.

326 BC
The Greek King Alexander the Great invades northern India.

321–184 BC
The Mauryan **Empire** spreads across northern India.

4th century AD
The Gupta Empire develops in southern India.

5–1279
The Chola Empire dominates southern India.

1206–1290
The Mamluk (Slave) **Dynasty** rules India. The Mamluks make Delhi their capital.

1216–1565
The Vijayanagara Empire is at its height in southern India.

1498
The Portuguese explorer Vasco Da Gama lands in India.

1526–1707
The Mughal Empire is at its height.

1600
The British East India Company starts trading in India.

1632–1654
Mughal Emperor Shah Jahan builds the Taj Mahal.

1757
First British Governor of Bengal, Colonel Robert Clive, defeats the Nawab of Bengal at the Battle of Plassey.

1853
First steam railway sets off from Bombay.

1857
Indian soldiers protest against British rule.

15 August 1947
India becomes independent. Jawaharlal Nehru becomes India's first prime minister.

1948
Mahatma Gandhi, who led India to independence, is assassinated.

1965
India wars with Pakistan.

1984
Prime Minister Indira Gandhi, Nehru's daughter, is assassinated.

1991
Prime Minister Rajiv Gandhi, Indira Gandhi's son, is assassinated.

2000
India's population reaches 1 billion.

dynasty series of rulers of the same family

India — Facts & figures

India's current flag was designed in 1947. It has three horizontal stripes — orange—yellow, white, and green.

People

- Population: 1.1 billion.
- One baby is born in India every 1.25 seconds.
- Average life expectancy: 63 years.

Money matters

- The average person in India earns about £300 US$500 in a year.
- The Indian railway system is the largest employer in the world. It employs over 1 million people.
- In 2004 it was estimated that 27 percent of the Indian population was living in poverty.

What's in a name?

- India's name comes from the valleys around the River Indus. This area was home to the early settlers.
- India's official name is Republic of India.

Food facts

- The term "curry" isn't really used in India. There are many types of curry-style dishes, which vary from region to region.
- You must only use your right hand for eating in India.

Glossary

Buddhism religion founded in India by Siddhartha Gautama in 525 B.C.E.

Buddhist to do with Buddhism or a follower of Buddhism

dynasty series of rulers of the same family

emblem object used as a symbol for a place, person, or thing

empire country or group of countries ruled over by another country

fertile good for growing crops and other types of plants

fort specially strengthened building designed to defend an area in wartime

habitat natural home of animals and plants

hill station small town or village high up in the hills

Himalayas mountain range in northeastern India. It extends into the countries of Nepal, Bhutan, and China.

Hindu to do with Hinduism or a follower of Hinduism

Hinduism religion that started in India. It involves the worship of many gods and goddesses.

holy associated with a divine power

Islam religion founded by the prophet Muhammad in the 7th century

monsoon rainy season, from June to August in India

monument important historic site or a structure built to honour a special person or event

mosque Muslim place of worship

Muslim to do with Islam or a follower of Islam

oxen male cattle

plain large, flat area of land

plateau area of flat land that is higher than the surrounding land

polluted when air, water, or soil has been made dirty or harmful by waste or chemicals

prophet person chosen by a god to tell people what the god wants them to do

reincarnation rebirth of the soul into another body

rickshaw small vehicle for carrying people and goods. Some are pulled by hand; others are pedalled or motorised.

Sikh to do with Sikhism or a follower of Sikhism. Sikhism is a religion based on the teachings of Guru Nanak.

sin bad deed against religious law

slum area populated by very poor people, where the conditions are dirty and overcrowded

starvation lack of basic food needed to survive

tribe group of people who live together and share the same language and customs

tsunami huge tidal wave caused by an earthquake or volcano

wisdom deep knowledge and good judgement

Index